THE INVESTOR'S GUIDE TO AN INFINITY OF TENANTS

Pierre Mouchette

Copyright © March 2018 by Pierre Mouchette

Published by: Real Property Experts LLC
PO Box 1593 | Fairfield, CT 06825 | USA

All rights reserved. No part of this publication may be reproduced or transmitted in any form or by any means, electronic or mechanical, including photocopying, recording, or any information storage and retrieval system, except as permitted under Section 107 or 108 of the 1976 United States Copyright Act, without the prior permission of the Publisher.

ISBN-13: 978-1986974479
ISBN-10: 1986974472

Printed in USA

This Real Property Experts LLC (RPE) publication is designed to provide accurate and authoritative information with regard to the subject matter covered. RPE publications are an educational source for investors and investment businesses. Content covers a range of investment business topics, including content related to *legal services, accounting, financing, taxes, insurance, management, and investment.*

Although, some of our writers and researchers hold credentials in law, real estate, and accounting, they and Real Property Experts LLC are not acting as licensed professionals. Our writers provide generally applicable content and try to break down complex topics so they are easier to understand. However, they are not providing specific advice for your business. Information that we provide may not apply to your specific situation, and products or services we rrecommend may not be a good fit for your particular investment business. While we strive to provide accurate up-to-date content, we cannot guarantee the accuracy and completeness of information that we provide. We regularly update articles, but it's possible that we may miss something. Use our content as a starting point to do your own research before selecting to use and choose a particular service or product for your investment business.

We recommend consulting your business attorney, accountant, tax professional, or other licensed professional for decisions that could affect your investment business legally or financially.

Contents

Chapter 1   HUD .... - 6 -
    Responsibilities .... - 6 -
    How It Works .... - 6 -
Chapter 2   THE PROGRAM .... - 7 -
    What Is The Program? .... - 7 -
    How Does It Work? .... - 7 -
    What Is The HAP Contract? .... - 7 -
    What Type Of Housing Is Acceptable For The Program? .... - 7 -
    Are There Any Down Sides To The Program? .... - 8 -
    Can An Applicant Be Denied A Rental? .... - 8 -
Chapter 3   THE PROPERTY OWNER .... - 9 -
    Tenant Selection .... - 9 -
    Approved Applicant .... - 10 -
    Pets .... - 11 -
    Tenant Warning .... - 11 -
    Terminating a Tenant .... - 11 -
    Disputes Between Tenants .... - 12 -
    Communications .... - 12 -
    Illegal Drugs .... - 13 -
    Lease Violation .... - 13 -
    Landlords Right to Disqualify an Applicant .... - 13 -
    Environmental Issues .... - 14 -
Chapter 4   TENANTS .... - 16 -
    RENTING TO SECTION 8 TENANTS .... - 16 -
    Concerns? .... - 16 -
    The Advantages Of Having Section 8 Tenants .... - 16 -
    SECTION 8 RULES for TENANTS .... - 18 -
    Tenant Responsibilities To Section 8 And To The Property Owner .... - 18 -

Chapter 5 RENTAL INSURANCE	- 20 -
Renter's Insurance	- 20 -
Why Does Your Tenant Need Renter's Liability Insurance?	- 20 -
Will Renter's Liability Insurance Cover The Tenant's Legal Fees?	- 20 -
What If The Has No Assets To Protect?	- 20 -
For Your Information	- 21 -
What You Should Know About Renters Liability Claims	- 21 -
Chapter 6 HOW MUCH DOES SECTION 8 PAY	- 22 -
How Much Will I Receive From The Housing Choice Voucher?	- 22 -
How Much Will The Tenant Contribute?	- 22 -
Chapter 7 RENT PAYMENT	- 24 -
Electronic Rent Payments	- 24 -
APPENDIX A	- 26 -
APPENDIX B	- 33 -

AUTHOR'S PREFACE

This booklet is designed to give you all the information you need and none of the information you do not need. In this booklet, we address the most pressing questions on how to obtain an infinity of tenants for the property owners rentals. We provide through the reading of this booklet how the property owner can advertise for free, acquire an unlimited number of tenants for free, and receive guaranteed rent each month. The booklet is full of simple, straight-forward, actionable facts with no fluff or unnecessary jargon.

Please take your time to read and apply the strategies herein to your rental investment business. In doing so, you will not arbitrarily perform a function but truly understand why it is done. Your actions will serve you, and others within your investment areas.

Pierre Mouchette, author

Chapter 1   HUD

Responsibilities

HUD is responsible for enforcing the Fair Housing Act of 1968, also known as Title VIII of the Civil Rights Act of 1968. Congress passed the act to impose a comprehensive solution to the problem of unlawful discrimination in housing based on race, color, sex, national origin, or religion.

How It Works

If a person feels they have been unfairly discriminated against, they can file a claim with HUD. It will notify the "alleged" offending party of the claim and allow them to respond. It will then determine if there is any merit to the claim.

HUD can offer the parties the ability to reconcile their complaint with a HUD Conciliation Agreement. If conciliation fails and HUD has "reasonable cause" to believe discrimination has occurred, the case will go to an administrative hearing or to Federal District Court if the parties prefer.

Chapter 2   THE PROGRAM

What Is The Program?

The Housing Choice Voucher Program is funded from federal funds received from the **U.S. Department of Housing and Urban Development (HUD),** and administered through local **Public Housing Agencies (PHAs)**. The program commonly referred to as **Section 8 Tenant Based Assistance**, provides *low-income tenants, seniors, or the disabled* with subsidized rental vouchers.

How Does It Work?

Individuals can use the vouchers to select the housing of their choice, if the property owner has agreed to accept the **HAP Contract.** The housing must also comply with the **PHA Health and Safety Codes.** The PHA will directly pay the property owner an agreed upon portion of the rent. The tenant is responsible for any additional rent that the voucher has not covered.

What Is The HAP Contract?

The Housing Assistance Program (HAP) Contract in its entirety can be reviewed online at HUD-5261 and HUD-5261-A. As stated above this contract is between the PHA and the property owner.

What Type Of Housing Is Acceptable For The Program?

Housing can be in the form of a single family residential, multifamily to a high-rise apartment building. No matter what type of housing the property owner has, before acquiring a **Section 8 Tenant,** the property must be inspected and approved. This inspection also known as the **Housing Quality Inspection** determines if your unit meets the **minimum housing standards** that have been set forth by HUD and the local PHA.

- if the unit fails to comply with any item on their lists of performance standards, the problem must be remedied within a set period. The unit must then be re-inspected before it can be approved for a Section 8 move-in.

- if the initial inspection is approved, Section 8 will allow the tenant to move-in. Additionally, Section 8 will perform an inspection once a year, usually when the tenant's lease is up for renewal.

Are There Any Down Sides To The Program?
The most commented on down-sides to the program are

- you cannot charge more than what HUD determines to be Fair Market Value (FMV) for the rental – you should take into consideration that your rent comes in on time every month, month after month

- the PHA does not always pay the entire rent, so the tenant is responsible for paying the difference – just check out the tenant and make sure that they can afford to make up the difference themselves (due diligence), or do not accept them

- your first rent payment is received after the tenant moves-into the property. Once your first payment arrives, you should expect consistent payments each month

- if you are going to increase the tenant's rent, you must submit a request form to the local PHA. The form usually asks what the current rent is, what the proposed rent will be, and the date that the new rent will become effective. You must also certify that the rent you are charging is not more than the rent that you are charging for any comparable units in your properties

Can An Applicant Be Denied A Rental?
Yes, do your standard application and credit check (due diligence).

Chapter 3 THE PROPERTY OWNER

Tenant Selection
To comply with all governing authorities, you must have a standard for tenant selection. This standard should be comprised of **Financials, Reliability, Stability,** and any other additional criteria that you may have. Do your due diligence by

- having an **Application Information** letter for the prospect to read and sign. This letter should at a minimum let them know that you only accept qualified tenants that are screened, that all application statements are verified, that a nationwide criminal background check will be performed, and that you comply with all Fair Housing Laws. See Figure A-2.

- your documentation should state that you have the right to verify at *any time* the information provided to you.

- you must verify all employment, banking, and emergency contact numbers.

- you must have a checklist with a point valuation system that each tenant is matched to. The applicant must obtain a minimum score so that you will not be brought-up on discrimination charges. See Figure A-1

- know the warning signs (credit report)
    o history of late payments - if the credit report reveals a history of late payments, you can expect your rent to be late too!
    o history shows lots of debt - verify that the applicant can afford to pay the rent!
    o low bank balances - this might indicate that the applicant lives month-to-month!
    o residency check - if the applicant moves a lot, this could be a warning sign!
- take digital photographs of the tenants, and their vehicles (showing their plates).

Note: *We recommend your research include:*

- *FBI Terrorist Watch List*
- *National Sex Offenders List*
- *Your State Sex Offenders List*

Approved Applicant
- once housing is selected by the prospective tenant and the PHA approves it, the family signs a lease (the terms of the lease are in accordance with all provisions of the HAP contract, and the lease includes the tenancy addendum) with the property owner (copy to PHA) for at least one year. The tenant may be required to pay a security deposit to the property owner (the PHA does not pay this). After the first year, the property owner may initiate a new lease or allow the family to remain on a month-to-month tenancy.

- rent payment: a housing subsidy is paid directly by the PHA on behalf of the participating family to the property owner. The family then pays the difference between the actual rent charged by the property owner and the amount subsidized by the program. The rent that the family pays is referred to as **Total Tenant Payment (TTP).** The TTP is determined by a formula developed by HUD and is based on the family's anticipated gross annual income less deductions. A copy of the **Housing Choice Voucher Guidebook** (7420.10G) is available on-line from HUD.

- termination of lease by owner - the owner may terminate the tenancy in accordance with the lease and HUD requirements. During the term of the lease or any extension term, the property owner may only terminate the tenancy because of
    - serious or repeated violation of the lease
    - violation of federal, state, or local law
    - criminal activity or alcohol abuse that threatens the health or safety of others
    - other causes such as - disturbance of neighbors; destruction of property; living or housekeeping habits that cause damage to the unit or premises

- after the initial lease term, such good causes include
    - the tenant's failure to accept the landlord's offer of a new lease or revision
    - the owner's desire to use the unit for personal or family use, or for a purpose other than a residential unit
    - business or economic reason for termination of the tenancy such as sale of the property, or renovation

If a property owner respects his tenants, they in turn will respect him. Mutual respect subrogates problems.

Pets

Today, more so than ever before, people have pets! Whether it is a dog or a cat, the animal possesses a symbiosis relationship that keeps us tranquil. As a property owner, having an animal on our property creates a multitude of problems

- if not attended to in a timely fashion, pet excrements can create permanent damage to the premises.
- dogs chew, and cats scratch surfaces if not trained.
- if left alone, the animal might create a nuisance through meowing, whining, and/or barking.
- they might jump on a neighbor in excitement and scare or injure them.

As a pet owner, finding affordable housing in a nice area that allows pets is very hard to achieve. Once found, the pet owner will most likely pay a *bounty* for the privilege of residency.

Tenant Warning

Sometimes good residents make mistakes, or things just happen. Whatever the reason, we give the tenant the benefit of doubt the first time with a warning letter. This letter serves as notice for the resident to get it together or get out!

Note: you must send a copy to the PHA

Terminating a Tenant

The Good - when a tenant has abided by the lease, but the neighbors have complained about them for various reasons

- document the complaints in writing from the complaining neighbor. Inform the offending tenant of the complaints and hope that they comply. If the issue becomes non-compliant after repeated notification send them a non-renewal letter and copy the PHA

The Bad - when tenants do not abide by the Lease (loud noise, drugs etc.) then it is time to take immediate action

- notify the PHA

- always start evictions immediately

- if the tenant has illegally kept possession of your property, they are stealing from you

Disputes Between Tenants

Whenever there are disputes between tenants, or just something that is unusual you should complete an Incident Report. This documentation will help you in the event of a tenant, or visitor property liability case, or for a future tenant eviction. Make sure that you put every complaint about a tenant in writing and keep it in the file. The document should have at a minimum

- when (date, day and time of the incident)
- what happened
- where did the incident happen (apartment, hallway, stair foyer, outside)
- how long did the problem continue
- who was involved
- were the police called (get a case number)
- who reported the information

Communications

It is of the utmost importance to have all communications with your tenants in writing. Even oral communications should be followed-up with a confirmation letter or e-mail. Keep a copy of the communiqué in the tenant's file. If you deliver letters personally by sliding them under the apartment door, note the date and time you did so on your copy, then place it in the tenant's file.

To comply with state, and local law you must communicate in writing with your tenants to give

- notice of intent to enter the premises
- notice of late rent payment
- notice of bounced check
- notice of violation of policy
- notice of lease expiration date
- notice that the lease will be increased, or not be increased
- other opportunities to communicate with your tenants are
    - to notify them of improvement work being performed on the grounds (give date and time schedule)

- o to inquire if recent repair to their apartment were completed to their satisfaction, and in a timely way
- o schedule a "Walk-thru Saturday" (they will be home), when you tighten door knobs, and oil the hinges
- o send holiday cards to all tenants thanking them for their tenancy
- o create a Newsletter that you publish quarterly letting the tenants know what is happening or coming up

Illegal Drugs

If you are aware that a tenant is involved in illegal drug-related activities on the premises, state laws require that you take all reasonable measures to evict the tenant as soon as it can be lawfully done. If you knowingly tolerate illegal drug activity on your property, you may be subject to a fine, and a prison sentence. You may also run the risk of your property being confiscated.

The law gives you some special remedies to evict a tenant quickly when illegal drugs are involved. You can begin immediate legal action against the offending tenant, without waiting for the standard notice requirements. You cannot evict the tenant without going to court.

Evicting a tenant for illegal drug activities requires proof that these activities are taking place on the premises. If you believe that illegal, drug activities are taking place you must go to the police. They can assure your safety and obtain evidence lawfully. You will need the police report for court.

Lease Violation

If you learn that a tenant is violating the lease, send the PHA and tenant and a letter or e-mail demanding that s/he cures the violation promptly. State in the letter that **any future rent will be accepted without waiving your right to insist that the violation be cured**. If your tenant can show a court that you accepted rent, month after month, while knowing of a lease violation, and without reserving your rights, the court may find that you have waived your right to complain about the lease violation.

Landlords Right to Disqualify an Applicant

Although a property owner may not discriminate against protected classes of individuals, a landlord may select prospective tenants based on any lawful **business criteria**. Property owners are free to set their own smoking, pet, and other policies if they are not discriminatory. Given the health risks and environmental issues associated with second hand smoke, increasingly property owners are excluding smokers from renting their property.

Note: HUD has launched a set of tools to encourage and guide owners to adopt smoke-free policies. This toolkit can be found at
http://portal.hud.gov/hudportal/HUD?src=/smokefreetoolkits1

A property owner may also reject an applicant based on the applicant's inability to pay rent. A valid occupancy policy limiting the number of people per rental unit (based on health and safety standards or local/state code) is a lawful basis for refusing an applicant to a specific rental unit.

Environmental Issues

Recent court decisions have held property owners responsible for the physical safety of their tenants, and their tenants' guest. Environmental issues are health issues. Some issues to be aware of are

- Lead Paint - lead was used as a pigment and drying agent in alkyd oil-based paint. This paint was used on interior and exterior surfaces but particularly on doors, windows, and other woodwork. In 1978 the use of lead was banned. The EPA, the Department of Housing and Urban Development (HUD) issued final regulations regarding lead, known as the Lead-Based Paint Hazard Reduction Act.

    o Landlords cannot refuse to rent to a family because there are known lead-based paint hazards in their property. This is considered discrimination. The landlord is responsible for providing the prospective tenant with the lead paint disclosure form, which will make the prospective tenant aware of any known hazards. The prospective tenant must then make their own decision about allowing their children to live in an apartment with known hazards.

- Asbestos - a fire-resistant mineral that was used to cover pipes, ducts, heating, and hot water units. Additionally, its fire-resistant properties made it a popular material for use in floor tiles, exterior siding, roofing products, linoleum flooring materials, joint compounds, wallboard materials, backing and mastics. In 1978 the use of asbestos was banned. Additional information can be obtained from the EPA.

- Radon - a naturally occurring, colorless, odorless, tasteless, radioactive gas produced by the decay of other radioactive substances. Fans and thermal stacks pull radon into the building through cracks in the buildings foundation. Radon has been classified as a "Class A" human carcinogen.

- Formaldehyde - a colorless chemical with a strong odor used in the manufacturer of building materials because of its preservative characteristics. Formaldehyde was listed as a hazardous air pollutant in the Clean Air Act Amendments of 1990. It is listed as a "probable human carcinogen." Formaldehyde may trigger respiratory problems (shortness of breath, wheezing, chest tightness, asthma) as well as eye and skin irritations. Additionally, it is a major contributor to Sick Building Syndrome.

- Mold - a fungus that can be found on any organic material so long as moisture, and oxygen are present. Mold causes biodegradation of natural materials, which can be unwanted when it becomes food spoilage or damage to property. Additionally, some molds can cause serious health problems by triggering allergic reactions and asthma attacks. Some molds are known to produce potent toxins and/or irritants. The EPA has published guidelines for the remediation and/or cleanup of mold.

- Building-Related Illness (BRI) - a clinically diagnosed condition that can be attributed to airborne building contaminants. Symptoms include asthma, hypersensitivity, and some allergies.

- Sick Building Syndrome (SBS) - n air quality condition caused by improper ventilation, and poor carpeting. Symptoms include fatigue, nausea, dizziness, headache, and sensitivity to odors.

Note: The local PHA will check for some or all of these environmental issues. It is your duty as a responsible property owner to take care of the above so that they will be non-existent in your properties.

Chapter 4   TENANTS

RENTING TO SECTION 8 TENANTS

Concerns?
There are some property owners who have major concerns about renting to Section 8 tenants. Of utmost concern is that the tenant will destroy their property, and in doing so will keep other 'quality' tenants from wanting to rent from them.

The Advantages Of Having Section 8 Tenants
Listing the advantages of having **Section 8 Tenants** are easy, and they are as follows

- **Consistent Rent Payments** – Section 8 is a government program that provides rental assistance. Applicants to the program who meet certain requirements are granted a housing voucher that allows them to look for housing within a certain price range. The program is administered by the local **Public Housing Authority (PHA)** who is responsible for paying the tenant's housing voucher directly to the property owner each month. The PHA will either mail the check or direct deposit the amount into the property owner's account.

    o Occasionally, a tenant is responsible for a small percentage of the rent and must pay this portion directly to the property owner each month. Section 8 tenants know that any violation of the terms of the lease agreement, including paying rent, could result in the loss of their Section 8 voucher. Therefore, they have a strong incentive to pay their portion of the rent each month.

- **Targeted Marketing** – your rental is advertised on and off-line

    o Online - Section 8 has a website that is dedicated *specifically* to Section 8 tenants. It is called Socialserve.com. You must first register online or by phone. Once registered, you are free to post any Section 8 friendly listings you have on the site. You can also inform your local PHA which may have their own online sites where you can also list your vacancy.

    o In Person - you can post flyers at the local PHA office. Additionally, the PHA has a master list of available Section 8 units that you can add your property to. This list can be viewed online or directly at the office as a hard-copy. This marketing method is a great way to reach those that may not have internet access. There is no cost for this service.

- **Consistent Tenant Base** – in having Section 8 tenants you are broadening your tenant base. There is high demand for Section 8 vouchers across the country. Many areas have wait lists of thousands of people. Even if your market does not have many tenants on Section 8, by accepting these tenants, you are not relying on them as the only way to fill your vacancy, but rather are increasing your prospective tenant pool.

- **Pre-Screened Tenants** – having Section 8 tenants means that the applicant has been pre-screened. The PHA screens for
    - income
    - criminal history
    - drugs – vouchers will not be provided to those that have been evicted due to drug related activities within the last three years

- **Disclosure** – the PHA is required to provide property owner's with the following information
    - type of screening they have conducted on the tenants
    - tenant's current and previous addresses
    - tenant's current and previous property owners

In making these disclosures to you, it does not relieve you of preforming your own due diligence, such as credit and background checks, sex offenders list, and terrorist list.

SECTION 8 RULES for TENANTS

Tenant Responsibilities To Section 8 And To The Property Owner

To receive and keep a Section 8 housing voucher, a tenant must follow certain rules. These requirements are in addition to any obligations the tenant already has under their state's landlord-tenant law. The Section 8 tenant must

Housing

- **Find a Section 8 Eligible Housing Unit** – the Section 8 office will pay the tenant's rent, but is not responsible for finding the tenant a unit to live in. The tenant must search on their own for housing within a specific town or county.

- Socialserve.com is a national Section 8 website where property owners can post units that accept Section 8 tenants. In addition, the local Section 8 office may have their own list or website where Section 8 tenants can view available rentals in the area.

- It is up to the tenant to make an appointment to view any properties they are interested in and to provide the landlord, and the Section 8 office with the necessary paperwork. Once the tenant has chosen a unit, the Section 8 office is responsible for inspecting the unit to determine if it meets **HUD's Housing Quality Standards**.

Pay Security Deposit

- The monthly vouchers that Section 8 tenants receive from the public housing agency do not include an amount for the security deposit. Therefore, the tenant is responsible for providing this deposit to the property owner.

- Tenants who have difficulty coming up with the security deposit on their own can apply to other assistance programs which may be able to help them pay the tenant's security deposit.

Pay Their Portion of the Rent

- While Section 8 pays most of a tenant's rent, it often does not pay all of it. The tenant can be responsible for paying a percentage of the rent based on their yearly income.

- The amount the tenant must pay on their own will vary from tenant to tenant. However, it is usually just a small portion of the rent.

- The tenant must pay their portion of the rent on time each month. Failure to pay their portion, or consistently paying late, may jeopardize the tenant's continued ability to receive a Section 8 voucher.

Follow the Lease Agreement Rules - Section 8 tenants must follow the terms of the lease agreement, or like any other tenant they can be evicted for breaching their lease agreement. They must follow the lease, including

- paying their rent on time
- keeping their unit clean
- not damaging the unit or property
- not disrupting the quiet enjoyment of other tenants in the building
- refraining from any criminal or illegal use of the property
- reporting any maintenance, health, or safety issues to the property owner

Notify Section 8 of Any Changes to Income or Family Size - The amount that the tenant receives from Section 8 depends heavily on both the household income and the size of the family. If there are any changes to either of these, the tenant is responsible for notifying the local PHA. Failure to notify Section 8 of changes could be considered fraud, and the tenant could lose their voucher entirely and even face legal action.

Notify Housing Authority and Landlord When Moving - When a Section 8 tenant wants to move out of a unit, they must not only notify their landlord, but they must also notify the local Section 8 office. Under normal circumstances, a Section 8 tenant can only move when their lease has expired or, for month to month leases, when giving the proper notice, either 30 or 60 days. For yearly leases, the tenant must give the property owner 30 days' notice prior to moving out. This notice is given so that the property owner has enough time to find a replacement tenant, and so that the housing authority knows when to stop lending the housing voucher to that property owner.

Chapter 5   RENTAL INSURANCE

Renter's Insurance

The tenant should be made aware of renter's insurance. Renter's insurance is an insurance policy that covers a renter's personal belongings in case of loss by fire, theft, or other accident. Renter's insurance also covers liability for claims or lawsuits brought against the renter. Most policies only cover personal property and do not include motor vehicles or animals. In addition, some policies exclude certain perils such as floods or earthquakes.

Why Does Your Tenant Need Renter's Liability Insurance?

A renter can be liable for injuries to their guest! In our litigious society, any number of things could potentially cause a lawsuit, from accidentally scalding someone with hot coffee, to leaving a pair of shoes on your stairwell that trips a guest on their way downstairs. Claims are filed annually for everything from serving alcohol to someone who later causes a car accident to severe dog bites.

Dog bites, account for about a third of home liability claims. Some renter's insurance policies will charge higher premiums to owners of dogs classified broadly as "dangerous breeds." Because of this many landlord's do not allow their tenants to have pets. If you own a dog, regardless if a pet is permitted in the lease, you can be held liable for medical and punitive costs if your dog happens to bite someone. If your dog destroys doors, screens and other property belonging to the rental property, you will typically be held liable for that damage as well.

Will Renter's Liability Insurance Cover The Tenant's Legal Fees?

Nearly all renter's liability policies include compensation for court costs and legal fees associated with a liability lawsuit. Your renter's liability insurance may not cover you if you willfully cause injury or damage. Be sure to check the details of the policy or ask an agent for clarification to fully understand what your coverage includes.

What If The Has No Assets To Protect?

Many people who have not built up personal wealth feel that liability insurance is unnecessary. It is important to know however, that in a serious legal claim, attorneys can go after assets you do not have. For example, even if you should file for bankruptcy, you may still be required to pay restitution. If you are sued and do not have the protection of liability coverage, your credit can be ruined, and your wages could be garnished for years to come. Renter's insurance is a very inexpensive way to prevent such a possibility.

For Your Information

Renter's insurance coverage shields you from having to pay out for any damages you accidentally cause to your apartment, the common building area where you reside, or any other resident's property. It also shields you if you are held responsible for injury to another person. Without renter's liability insurance to shield you from unexpected accidents, you could lose your apartment and be liable for thousands of dollars in damages.

Your renter's policy provides coverage on **named perils** (the events that a renter's insurance policy identifies as covered) basis which includes loss due to *fire, lightening, windstorm, explosion, smoke, glass breakage, theft, hail, and more.* The renter's policy also includes liability coverage for accidental physical injury or damage to property brought about by the insured.

The **liability only insurance option** provides coverage against accidental physical injury and/or damage to property brought about by the insured. This option does not provide for any contents coverage.

Note: This is a general description of coverages for informational purposes only. Please refer to the actual policy for terms, conditions, exclusions, and limitations.

What You Should Know About Renters Liability Claims

Here are a few statistics to consider regarding renter liability claims that might happen in your apartment or rental home

- the average cost of dog-bite claims was $37,000
- on average, the cost of slip-and-fall accidents exceeds $22,000
- the cost of legal defense in a slip-and-fall lawsuit is $50,000

As you can see, costs associated with seemingly minor accidents around apartments and rental homes can come with a very high price tag. Having insurance coverage in place will protect your tenant from shouldering the cost of medical expenses or legal fees completely out of pocket.

Chapter 6   HOW MUCH DOES SECTION 8 PAY

How Much Will I Receive From The Housing Choice Voucher?
If you are willing to accept tenants who receive housing choice vouchers, you must understand how the voucher amount is calculated. No matter what your rental could receive in the open market, it does not mean the program will be willing, or able to pay you that same amount. The maximum amount that you will receive from the PHA is based on a variety of factors, such as

- Fair Market Value (FMV) - each year, HUD calculates the FMR for over 2,500 areas of the country. When calculating this number, HUD considers all units that have been rented in that specific area over the last 15 months. It excludes units that are less than two years old, assisted living units or other units that have been rented at what they consider to be below-market rent.
    - HUD uses two bedrooms as the standard for calculating FMV. It then derives the rents for all other bedroom sizes from the FMR for the two bedrooms

    - The FMV is set at a level that is in the 40th percentile for the rents in the area. This means that 40-percent of the units in the area rented for less than this amount and 60-percent of the units in the area rented for more than this amount. Therefore, it is slightly lower than the median rents for the area. The FMR for certain metropolitan areas will be set at the 50th percentile instead of the 40th percentile

- Payment Standard – the local PHA will then use the FMV that HUD has set as a guide. The PHA will look at factors in their area such as, how long it takes a family to locate housing, and will determine their payment standard, or the maximum amount they are willing to pay for each number of bedrooms. This payment standard will be between 90 and 110 percent of the FMR.

How Much Will The Tenant Contribute?
Tenants who receive housing choice vouchers must contribute a tenant portion to the rent. The amount that the tenant must contribute will be the greater of

- 30-percent of their monthly adjusted income
- 10-percent of their monthly gross income
- the welfare rents

- or the minimum rent amount set by the PHA

The tenant portion will be paid directly to the property owner by the tenant. If the rent for the unit is set at a higher amount than the payment standard the PHA has set for the unit, the tenant can elect to pay more. They can increase their tenant portion if the amount they will pay is approved by the PHA and does not account for more than 40-percent of the tenant's monthly adjusted income.

Utility Allowance - if utilities are included in the monthly rent, the PHA will usually include an amount for utilities when issuing the housing choice voucher. If the rent for the unit does not include utilities, the PHA may issue the tenant a separate amount for utility allowance or may issue a utility reimbursement directly to the tenant or directly to the utility company.

Chapter 7   RENT PAYMENT

Electronic Rent Payments
Having your tenant pay their rent electronically is the best way for both you, and your tenant to have this monthly chore accomplished. Using an electronic payment service company will save you from the burdensome task of sending reminders, late payment notices, and late fees.

Your tenants can pay their rent by a modern-day system that is designed for them. In using this system, they will

- save time and money (postage, envelopes, and checks)
- ensures that they pay on time (debts are automatic, tenants with an email address receive advance notification of the upcoming debit)
- the system can align debit days with paydays

They can pay

- online
- through a mobile application
- through automatic payments (credit or debit card). Some tenants like the fact that a credit card is available for this transaction since their bank account may be short one month, and using the card ensures continuity, avoids late charges, and keeps their credit intact

Additional benefits that you as property owner enjoy are

- you have access to detailed records (real-time and historical) through the service providers **Dashboard.** The Dashboard is accessible through desktop or mobile devices. You can see invoices and who has paid, and how much. You can see monthly breakdowns by apartment, building, and invoice
- The Service Company handle all reminders and notifications. You can track these notifications through the systems Dashboard
- tenants can be invoiced for utilities, additional rent, and additional services requested. Invoices are created on-line by you, one-time or recurring
- collecting late payments is a fact of business for property owners. You cannot prevent this but, the electronic payment service company can set

the amount to charge them either by percentage or dollar amount. This can be accomplished by automatically cut-off dates that you select

- an email can be sent to you informing you of deposits to your account

Using an electronic payment service company is not free. The cost of this service is well worth the alternatives. Service cost can be absorbed by you or paid by the tenant. For more information on these service companies see APPENDIX B

If the primary method you use to collect rental payments is online, you usually have to allow another form of payment for those that do not have access to online resources, such as paying rent by mail.

APPENDIX A

Figure A-1

Sample: Non-Bias (Minimum Resident Standard) Form

NON-BIAS (MINIMUM RESIDENT STANDARD)
MINIMUM CRITERIA AND CHECKLIST FOR RESIDENT SELECTION

Automatic disqualification for an apartment.

	The apartment applied for is in a non-smoking building and the applicant(s) smoke.
	The building is a non-pet building and the applicant has a pet(s).
	Incomplete application.
	Applicant lied on application.
	Eviction for non-payment or cause.
	Case for property damage, disturbances, nuisance, foreclosure, or other.
	Four or more 30-day delinquencies; Three or more 60-day delinquencies. Any combination of four 30-day or 60-day delinquencies.
	One 90-day or greater delinquency, charge-off, collection, skip, or civil suit.
	Any repossession, tax lien, or bankruptcy.

Give a score of one point (or more when applicable) for each of the following criteria. Add up the total points to see if the applicant reaches the minimum acceptable score.

Financial Criteria	
	Minimum score on credit report of 650. (Add 1 point for each additional 10 points over 650; deduct 1 point for each 5 points below 650).
	Sufficient income (monthly income is 3 times the rent amount.)
	Sufficient income (monthly income is more than 4 times the rent amount.)
	Verifiable source of income of employment.
	Same source of income for a minimum of 1 year. (2 years = 2 points; 3 years = 3 points, etc. up to a maximum of 5 points.) Must provide W2s for proof of income.
	Able to pay full deposit and rent requested.
	Currently paying comparable amount of rent.
	No negative remarks on credit report.
	No late payments in past 6 months on credit report.
	No excessive financial obligations (more than 50% of income.)
	Has a checking account.
	Has a savings account.
	Able to provide 3 Credit references.
	No late notices from current landlord.
	No prior evictions.
	Able to provide a cosigner. (2 points if cosigner owns real estate.)

____   **Total** (maximum 40 points this section).

Rental Stability Criteria

	Resided at current address minimum of 1 year. (2 years = 2 points; 3 years = 3 points, etc. up to a maximum of 5 points.) Must have been responsible for rent payment.
	No health or safety violations present upon inspection of current residence.
	No security deposit to be withheld because of property upkeep at current residence.
	No notices of any kind from current landlord regarding a rental agreement violation.
	No neighborhood complaints of residents or pets, or police reports on disturbing the peace.
	No pets.
	Good report from the landlord prior to the current landlord
	No criminal history.

_____ **Total** (maximum 15 points this section).

Additional Criteria

	Move-in date within an acceptable time period.
	Personal appearance and automobile appearance is neat and clean.
	Will have rent payments electronically paid each month. (add 10 points)

_____ **Total** (maximum 15 points this section).

_____ **Total Criteria Points**

Applicant's Total Score

Date of Application:		Date Verified:	
Above Criteria Verified by:		Applicant Notified	☐ acceptance ☐ denial
Action Taken:		By what method:	
Date Applicant Notified:			
Any other action required:			

To be sure that you do not discriminate against any person, please follow the above minimum standard for tenant selection. The applicant who scores highest over the minimum should be selected in order to conform to this non-bias form.

All applicants who do not score above the minimum criteria can be disqualified. Adverse letter required to comply with Fair Credit Reporting Act (FCRA).

Figure A-2

Sample: Application Information Letter

Application Information

Dear Rental Applicant

We take pride in our rental apartments and we actively seek only qualified tenants to reside in them. We screen our applicants carefully, and we completely verify all information provided to us on the rental application. We run a credit report on every applicant, a criminal background check, employment verification, and we check previous rental history.

The screening and verification process is used for every applicant the same way - **fairly and consistently.** We are in compliance with the **Fair Housing Laws** at all times. An applicant who passes the screening criteria is offered a tenancy when one is available. An applicant who does not satisfy the screening criteria is not accepted as a tenant. If there are more than one applicant for the same rental, the most qualified applicant will be accepted.

By making an application for one of our rentals, you acknowledge that these verifications will be completed and give us permission to do them. Please completely fill in the rental application. If you do not provide us with complete information, we will not be able to process the application. We will do our best to process your application quickly (normally within a 72-hour period). If you have not heard back from us by then, feel free to contact us. Please read and sign below acknowledging acceptance of the terms of your application. Thank you for making an application for one of our rentals and we hope you will become a long-term resident with us.

1. I have double-checked the information I have provided on the rental application and agree that it is true and complete.

2. I understand that an annual update of the information on this application may be requested. I agree to provide updated information and notify management of any changes (i.e., employment, phone number, bank, car, emergency contact.)

3. My credit report/history is good. If not, I have attached a separate page to explain my credit problems.

4. I understand and agree that this application is subject to approval based on the information on my application. If any of the information I have given turns out to be FALSE, my application will be denied.

5. I understand and agree that this application is NOT a lease or rental agreement, and should it be accepted, I will sign the lease provided within FIVE business days of being accepted. Should I fail to do so, the application shall be considered withdrawn. There will be no further obligation to reserve the rental, and my holding deposit will be forfeited.

6. I hereby waive any claim for damages if my application is not accepted.

7. I understand that every good faith effort will be made to have the premises ready for occupancy as promised. However, should the premises not be available for occupancy on the date promised, I hereby waive any and all rights to seek to recover damages of any kind from the Landlord or Management Company.

8. I hereby authorize and permit the Landlord and/or Management Company to obtain any information necessary to verify the accuracy of any information or statements I have made on this application. I authorize and permit my credit report to be obtained and further authorize the Landlord or Management Company to make further credit inquires in regard to continued credit worthiness and for purposes of collection of unpaid rent or damages to premises, should that become necessary.

9. I permit upon occasion, contact with my employer to verify my employment status during my tenancy.

10. I shall not hold the Landlord or Management Company responsible for any allergic reactions to the premises, inside or outside, from me, other occupants, or guests. I shall check for allergic reactions before signing the Lease Agreement.

11. I certify that I am not manufacturing, using, storing, or selling dangerous controlled substances and understand that I will immediately be required to vacate the premises, if evidence of such is found on the premises, or if I am convicted of any crimes related to possession and/or distribution of controlled, dangerous substances.

12. I further understand and agree that the security deposit and first month's rent must be paid in full by **Money Order** or **Teller's Check** before moving in. If I am unable to or fail for whatever reason to pay the balance of the amount due at that time, the application shall be considered withdrawn, and my holding deposit will be forfeited.

By: _____ _____ _____
    (applicant's signature)   (applicant to print name)   (date)

By: _____ _____ _____
    (applicant's signature)   (applicant to print name)   (date)

Figure A-3
_____

Sample: Letter of Acceptance

date

name

street

city, state, zip

This letter confirms our conversation on   {*date*}   at   {*time*} , in which you accepted our offer to rent the apartment at   {*rental property address*}   . As we discussed, these are the rental terms:

Rent $ Deposit $

Rental start date: 20_____

Rental term: 1 Year   Lease, ending on   20_____

Number of occupants: _____

NO PETS

_____

Deposit and first month's rent total $ to be paid by <u>Cashier's Check</u> or <u>Money Order</u> on or before _____ 20_____ at this address   *landlord's address*

Holding deposit of ___*[amount]*___ to be paid by ___*[date]*___ at this address _____.

We will sign the rental documents on ___*[date]*___ at ___*[time]*___ at ___*[address]*___.

_____

Thank you for deciding to live here. I look forward to working with you to ensure that your move in and tenancy are smooth and enjoyable. If you have any questions, please don't hesitate to call me.

Yours truly,

_____

Landlord (Property Owner)

Figure A-4
_____

Sample: Welcome New Resident

Welcome New Resident

We hope that you will enjoy your new home. To assist you in being settled, we would like to take this opportunity to explain some of our services, and the property's policies, procedures and rules.

LANDLORD

The Landlord maintains the following schedule:	Monday thru Friday	10:00 A.M.	to	4:00 P.M.
	Saturday	10:00 A.M.	to	2:00 P.M.
	Sunday	Closed		Closed

If you have any problem or need any information about your residence please feel free to call us at (   ) **XXX-XXXX**

PAYMENT OF RENT

Rents are due in full on the first day of the month.

Make rent checks payable to:

Mail checks to:

Your rent becomes delinquent on the 10th day of the month. Payments not received by the 10th of the month are subject to a $50.00 late charge (and an additional $1.00 for each subsequent day until the delinquent rent is paid.) You may also make a cash payment to the landlord to stop additional penalties.

MAINTENANCE

You are responsible for the routine upkeep of your residence. You are responsible to make all necessary repairs costing less than $150.00. To request service, please contact the (Landlord; Property Manager; Resident Manager) during normal working hours. If an emergency occurs when the office is closed, please call: (   ) XXX-XXXX

Management is responsible for maintenance and repairs necessitated by normal wear and usage. Repair of damage caused by resident negligence or misuse is the responsibility of the resident. In such cases, the maintenance staff will make the repairs, but the resident will be charged for the cost of labor and materials.

APPENDIX B

Commonly Used Words and Phrases

Arbitration - using a neutral third party to resolve a dispute instead of going to court.
Agreement - an exchange of promises, a mutual understanding or arrangement, a contract. *All agreements must be in writing and acknowledged by all parties.*
Common Area - areas generally accessible to all residents or users, such as hallways, stairs, laundry rooms, and yards.
Consumer Report - a detailed report that provides personally identifiable information relating to credit, character, or lifestyle.
Consumer Reporting Agency - an entity that collects and disseminates information about consumers to be used for credit evaluation.
Default - a tenant's failure to do something that the lease requires or that the law requires.
Default Judgment - a judgment issued by a court, without a hearing, when the tenant has failed to file a response to the landlord's complaint.
Discrimination - denying a person housing or stating that housing is not available because of a person's race, color, religion, sex, sexual orientation, national origin, ancestry, age, disability, or marital or familial status. Treating people differently could be considered discrimination.
Eviction - court proceeding for removing a tenant from a rental because the tenant violated the rental agreement or did not comply with a notice ending the tenancy.
Executed contract - contracts that are signed by all parties. *Sometimes referred to as signed in counterpart.*
Fees - money collected from tenants that will not be returned at the end of the tenancy (applicant screening, pets, cleaning, etc.).
Guest - a person who does not have the rights of a tenant but stays in/on the premises for a set period.
Housing Assistance Program (HAP) - temporary (2+ years) housing subsidy with private landlords: singles, duplexes, multi-family, and apartment buildings. Participants must move onto a more permanent housing subsidy after 2-years, such as the Housing Choice Voucher Program.
Housing Choice Voucher (HCV) - The housing choice voucher program is the federal government's major program for assisting very low-income families, the elderly, and the disabled to afford decent, safe, and sanitary housing in the private market. Since housing assistance is provided on behalf of the family or individual, participants are able to find their own housing, including single-family homes, townhouses and apartments. The participant is free to choose any housing that meets the requirements of the program and is not limited to units located in subsidized housing projects. Housing Choice Vouchers are administered locally by public housing agencies (PHAs). The PHAs receive federal funds from the U.S. Department of Housing

and Urban Development (HUD) to administer the voucher program.
Inspection Checklist - a written checklist or statement specifically describing the condition and cleanliness of or existing damages to the premises and furnishings.
Lessee - the tenant.
Lessor - the property owner.
Rental Criteria - a set of written standards that an applicant must meet in order to qualify for tenancy. By having these criteria, you are applying your rental selections consistently and fairly to avoid fair housing issues.
Section 8 - a federally funded government program. The U.S. Department of Housing and Urban Development (HUD) regulates the Section 8 program, while the local Housing Authority administers the program at the local level. It is designed to assist very low-income families, the elderly and the disabled to rent decent, safe and sanitary housing. A housing subsidy is paid directly to the landlord on behalf of a participating family.
Tenant - one or more persons who are given possession of real estate for a fixed period of time or at will. Synonym: occupant, resident.
Tenant Screening - a process used by property owners to evaluate prospective tenants to ascertain if the applicant will fulfill the terms of the rental agreement. The process culminates in a decision as to whether to approve the applicant conditionally (such as requiring a cosigner) or deny tenancy.
Walk-through - a final inspection of the house by the buyer to check for any last-minute problems that must be addressed. These items are recorded on a 'punch list.'

Electronic Rent Payment Companies

Note: Each company listed below offers different levels of service. Please review their offering on their website.

ClearNow, Inc. 115 Market Street Suite 360A Durham, NC 27701	Clearnow.com/ (866) 882-5327 (919) 680-4700
eRentPayment	eRentpayment.com/ (303) 459-4990 Toll Free: (866) 852-5366 Fax: (866) 373-7591
PayClix 989 W. Kennedy Blvd. Suite 101 Orlando, FL 32810	payclix.com (866) 729-2549
PayLease	payLease.com/ (866) 729-5327
PayYourRent 14488 Old Stage Road Lenoir City, TN 37772	Payyourrent.com/ (888) 800-4797
Rams Rent 2541 Barrington Circle Suite 2 Tallahassee, FL 32308	ramsrent.com/ (888) 944-RAMS Fax: (888) 523-9655
Rent Merchant 400 S. Street Suite 500 Las Vegas, Nevada 89101	rentmerchant.com (888) 427-1597
Rent Monitor 206 6th Avenue Des Moines, IA 50309	Rentmonitor.com/ (844) 476-8668
RentShare 115 E 23rd St 5th Floor New York, NY 10010	rentshare.com/landlord (888) 407-5023
True Rent 777 Woodside Road Redwood City, CA 90461	sublet.com

INFORMATION SERVICES

Advantage Tenant
800-894-9047
www.AdvantageTenant.com

*

Citi Credit Bureau
800-710-2484
www.Citicredit.net

*

The National Landlord Tenant Guides
www.RentLaw.com

*

Validus Information Services
www.ValidUSInfo.com

*

You Check Credit.com
www.youcheckcredit.com

*

Tenant Alert
866-272-8400
www.tenantalert.com

*

Tenant Verify
www.tenantverify.com

*

Tenant Background Search

www.TenantBackGroundSearch.com

THE INVESTOR'S GUIDE TO AN INFINITY OF TENANTS

Pierre Mouchette – Real Estate Investment Author

Pierre Mouchette is the Founder and CEO of Real Property Experts LLC. He is a graduate from New York University 1971, with a Master's in Business Administration, a Certificate in Real Estate Law - Fairfield University, Connecticut and held licensing as a Real Estate Broker, and Mortgage Broker.

For a complete outline of Pierre's Education, Experience and Recognition see https://realpropertyexperts.biz/team.html

Pierre has an extensive background in real estate investment, business management and sales, supplemented by decades of hands-on-experience in building systems engineering, development, evaluation and assorted analytical engineering studies.

Using background knowledge and experience, Pierre launched Real Property Experts in 2013 to help simplify real estate investing by connecting investors through innovative technology. Pierre authors Books, Booklets, How-to-Articles, and Guides to help investors make knowledgeable informed decisions.

Recommended Reading

The Multifamily Buyer's Manual
The Art of "Purchasing Right" Your Multifamily Home Investment

The Art of Being The Landlord
How to be a Landlord

The Team
Creating and Building Your Business Team

Cash Flow
How to determine if your property is cash flowing.

A Guide To Renter's Insurance
A complete informational as to why a tenant must have renter's insurance.

www.ingramcontent.com/pod-product-compliance
Lightning Source LLC
Chambersburg PA
CBHW062235220526
45471CB00009B/3490